TH
GEORDIE NETTY

A SHORT HISTORY AND GUIDE

by

FRANK GRAHAM

ISBN 0 946928 08 8

© 1986

First published by Frank Graham
Published by Butler Publishing in 1986

Published by BUTLER PUBLISHING
Thropton, Rothbury, Northumberland NE65 7LP

Printed by Mayfair Printers Ltd.

A fine study by Robert Olley

An Artistic Geordie netty. These netties were once very popular among Geordie intellectuals. Their production was subsidised by Northern Arts.

Following the cholera epidemic at Sunderland in 1831 there was considerable agitation about the state of sanitation in the town. A letter from William Knott in December 1840 stated:— I beg respectfully to make known to you a serious existing abuse viz: — the fact that the street lamps are extinguished generally two or three hours before daylight at this time of the year which is a source of considerable danger . . . there are some awkwardly-situated public privies adjoining the river; four men have been drowned within a short space of time when going to these early in the morning, the lamps being out at the time; and I know, from personal observations, that individual collisions, and consequent brawls, are of frequent occurrence."

A sanitary report for 1848 describes "a very great public nuisance existing at the east end of Broad Street, being a very large public privy, containing many cart-loads of night-soil. Near to, but not adjoining these, were two privies in a yard, constructed with two flaps or hatches at the top, so that as the soil accumulates it forces these hatches open."

THE MEDIEVAL GARDEROBE

Northumberland has many very ancient lavatories in the scores of old castles which survive. They are called "garderobes" a euphemism often confused with "wardrobe". They were usually built near the bedchamber although during the night the chamber pot was normally used. The place preferred was in the wall or in a buttress but where they were not sufficiently thick they were built out on corbels. Our illustration shows a fine example at Aydon Castle near Hexham. The privy itself is a small oblong apartment with a barrel vaulted roof with the bastion like projection acting as exit.

Usually the privies emptied on to a moat, river or precipice. The shaft was sometimes long and reached to the ground, a dangerous practice since it allowed possible although uncomfortable access to an enemy. The smell from castle netties was pretty strong and Henry III sent the following message ahead when he was coming to London:—

Since the privy chamber in London is situated in an undue and improper place, wherefore it smells badly, we command you on the faith and love by which you are bounden to us that you in no wise omit to cause another privy chamber to be made in such more fitting and proper place that you may select there, even though it should cost a hundred pounds . . .

For toilet paper the Romans used a sponge but in the castles of the north in the Middle Ages hay was the normal material.

Hail Cloucina goddess of this place,
The votary of every child of Grace,
Soft on thy seat may our oblations flow,
Not rudely swift nor obstinately slow.

LARN YERSEL GEORDIE

by SCOTT DOBSON

4

Many writers at the time and since have remarked upon the "rustic crudities" of some of Bewick's tail-pieces. The wood engraving of a Geordie netty offended most of his middle class contemporaries just as much as his left-wing political views. Ruskin in a letter confessed his "perpetually increasing wonder at the fixed love of *ugliness* in the British soul which renders the collective works of three of our greatest men—Hogarth, Bewick and Gruikshank,—totally unfit for the sight of women and children, and fitter for the furniture of gaols and pig-styes than of the houses of gentlemen and gentlewomen".

Ruskin's wealthy house in London was so far removed from the simple homes of the Northumbrian workers and farm labourers that he was totally unable to see Bewick's humour. We here reproduce the two engravings (the first as far as I know has never been published again since Bewick's time). The bowdlerized version appeared in the second edition of "Land Birds".

LOW HAUXLEY WHEEL-BARROWS

The interesting netties at Low Hauxley have been photographed by Mr. A. Jenson. Here is his description:—

"This village is only one or two feet above sea level, and the houses are about 20 yards from the sea water. The method of operation was this. The barrow was taken to the beach and about six inches of sand put in; then taken back to the toilet, and additional sand was added when used. At the end of the week it was taken to the beach and emptied, and refuse was washed away with the tide. The village has no drains as we know them, as it is too low in relation to the sea. Now most of the toilets of the 30 houses have been converted to chemical toilets. You will note that some newcomers to the village used the barrows for decoration and plants."

Low Hauxley is a village which is under danger from the sea. However a local authority sewage scheme is under way, presumably employing a pump, and may now be operational.

DRUNK IN CHARGE OF A NETTY

Have you heard of the Geordie who made a claim to his insurance company because his car had been hit and damaged by a mobile netty which was being towed from a sporting event. The driver was charged with being drunk in charge of a lavatory.

A strange contraption from Beamish
No prize for discovering how it works

Euphemism for an outside lavatory used by Country snobs:—
Gardener's toilet.

In Italy a row of toilets is called *Gabinetti.* Is this the origin of
the Geordie *netty*? Does the name go back to the Roman occupation.

Yesterday thieves broke into the South Shields Police Station and
stole the toilets. Police say they have absolutely nothing to go on.

Report Shields Gazette

SUNDERLAND CHAMBER POTS

In the 19th century the Sunderland potteries turned out millions of pieces each year. Most of it was pink lustre-wave, transfer printed. They were manufactured for a working class market both at home and abroad. Much of it was humorous, vulgar but full of life. Their frog mugs are famous and common but chamber pots are rare. I only know of two examples one of which is illustrated here. It was made at the "Garrison Pottery". The other example was rather sombre with the following inappropriate rhyme.—

> Swiftly see each moment flies,
> See and learn be timely wise,
> Every moment shortens day,
> Every pulse beats life away,
> Thus thy every heaving breath,
> Wafts thee on to certain death,
> Seize the moments as they fly,
> Know to live and learn to die.

The pottery was the same. They probably made this for the middle class customers who wanted moral thoughts when they went to relieve themselves.

IN THE MONASTERY

Here the garderobe (or *necessarium* or reredorter) with its rows of seats had no flushing water but usually emptied into a stream. Towels were left in a recess and in one of our monasteries the brethren "were not to blow their noses on the towel or to remove dirt with them".

One of Bewick's tailpieces

"*Fairings*", like the one above, were once very popular
ornaments

"Suitable for reading but bad for health. The superiority of the
Geordie race and their great achievements owe much to our
netties."

Anonymous

"The seats are made of one piece of wood and are round or oval
with a hole in the centre."

Archaeological report

The books read: HISTORIC NEWCASTLE £5, CASTLES OF NORTHUMBERLAND £6, The Geordie Laff In 50p, BEWICK'S MEMOIRS £350

A Geordie bibliophile had a stool made up of his favourite books. It was camouflage for a unique commode.

SEATON DELAVAL HALL

Since it was built by Vanburgh in 1721 Delaval Hall has been plagued by draughts. John Dobson tried to remedy this defect but with little success. Although the hall was cold the toilets were really comfortable. They were outside—perhaps to eliminate smell—and Susan Martin shows what they are like today. You can guess which was the ladies and which the gents entrance. Near the toilets is a fine old ice house in a good state of preservation.

"WeeLoc Netty"

Two fine decorated Victorian lavatory pans from the Beamish Museum. Although 100 years old and used thousands of times they are in prime condition due to the loving care and superb craftsmanship with which they were manufactured.

SIMONBURN RECTORY

Probably the finest old toilet in Northumberland is the three-seater at Simonburn Rectory. The date is probably early 18th century. One of the three is a child's lavatory. The three-seater is at the bottom of the garden in a fine stone building. Our drawing by Susan Martin shows the rector making his late night visit.

The old two seater lavatories are now becoming very rare. Apart from the ones mentioned in this book the only others I know in Northumberland are at Roses Bower Farm and at Spindlestone near Belford.

The march of "progress"
Interior of the Simonburn toilet above and a six compartment 20th century public convenience below.

Strange to say there are few jokes about netties. However Dick Irwin has provided us with some.

GEORDIE GETS THE BRUSH OFF

There was a knock on Geordie's door one day, standing on the step was a brush salesman. "Good morning sir", he says, "Would your good lady like any brushes?" "Well ye've come on a bad day son", says Geordie, "The wife's gone for a fortnight, she's staying with her sister in Blyth". "Not to worry", says the salesman, "I'll leave three samples, the wife can have a look at them, I'll call back in three weeks". So he left a clothes brush, a sweeping brush and a hedgehog with a handle on (toilet brush). Three weeks to the day the salesman called back at Geordies house. "Good morning", he said "Did your wife like any of the samples I left?" "Why I'll be honest". says Geordie, "She liked that claes brush, she thinks that sweeping brush is clivor, but she cares nowt for that lavotary brush, she'd sooner have the paper".

GEORDIE WESHINGTON

Sep Walker was varry proud of his netty doon at the bottom of the garden, with the burn running past it. Till one sad day Sep's netty was pushed into the burn. The irate Sep grabbed his son Tucker. "Listen lad", he says, "Did ye push that netty in the burn?" "No fethor", says young Tucker, "I didn't!" "Sit doon son", says Sep. "I'll tell ye a story. Once upon a time there was a lad caaled Geordie Weshington and he chopped he fethor's cherry tree doon. When his fethor got in from back shift he says to young Geordie, 'Did ye chop that cherry tree doon?' 'Why fethor', says young Geordie, 'I canna tell a lie, yes I chopped the cherry tree doon.' So instead of giving him a good belting, his fethor forgave him cos he'd told the truth. Noo I'll ask you again, did ye or did ye not push that netty in the burn?" "Fethor!" says young Tucker. "After hearing that story I've got te tell the truth, I pushed the netty in the burn". Why Sep picks him up, lays him ower his knee, took off his belt and gave young Tucker the biggest howking he'd ivor had. Tucker's blairing his eyes oot, "Fethor! Why did you giv iz a hiding, when I told ye the truth? Geordie Weshington's fethor forgave him when he told the truth aboot the cherry tree." "Aye I knaa", says Sep. "But Geordie Weshington's fethor wasn't sitting in the cherry tree at the time".

A married couple viewed a house in the country. On returning home they remembered that they had not noticed the W.C. So they wrote to the vicar who had shown them round the house asking him if he knew where the W.C. was. Being ignorant of the term the vicar thought they meant Wesleyan Chapel. So imagine their surprise when they received the following letter.

Dear Sir and Madam
    I regret to inform you that the nearest W.C. in the district is five miles away. This is rather unfortunate if you are in the habit of going regularly. It may interest you to know that many people take their lunch to make a day of it. By the way it is built to accomodate 1,000 and it has been decided to replace the old wooden seats with plush ones to ensure greater comfort especially to those who have to sit a long time before the proceedings begin. There are those who have time to walk, others go by train and get there just in time. I myself *never go*.

    There are special facilities for ladies provided by the ministers who give them all the assistance they need. The children sit together and sing through the proceedings. The last time my wife was there (that was twelve months ago) she had to stand all the time.

    Hoping this will be of use to you and trusting you will be able to go regularly.

I am yours faithfully,
The Vicar

P.S. Hymn sheets are provided free and are hanging behind the door.

Geordie had a big win at the races. They decided to instal an indoor nettie. When the work was finished his wife suggested they hold a party for the neighbours in the back yard. The celebrations went off well and when it was all over Geordie was sitting on a box exhausted with his head between his friends. His mate asked what was the matter. Geordie said he was just thinking what a strange world it was. "We used to have our grub in the house and gan down the yard to the nettie. Now we have money we have our grub in the yard and gan into the house for the nettie".

Two fine urinals in cast iron. They are described as of great strength and solidity with the cast iron plates dovetailed and jointed together in a neat manner.

"The exterior is ornamented by light scroll work, a new treatment of cast iron that is very effective. It is lighted from the sides by the open fretwork below the gutter cornice, and at night by lamps in the roof. A thorough system of ventilation is provided by means of effluvia pipes and the open fretwork.

SOME STATISTICS

The modern water closet was invented many years ago by one Mr. Crapper and he has often been blamed for western man's major physical problem—censtipation. Lately Professor Alexander Kira of Cornell University has produced a 255 page tome suggesting how the defects in Mr. Grapper's system can be overcome. It is a monumental work and a mine of information. For example we learn that the faeces (shit) of an average adult is between 4 to 8 inches long and from $\frac{5}{8}$ inch to $1\frac{7}{8}$ inches wide, weighing between $3\frac{1}{2}$ to 7 ounces. There is no historical evidence available to show whether the Geordies of the 19th century conformed to these standard measurements. The faeces consists of 65 per cent water, 10 to 20 per cent ash, 10 to 20 per cent solubles and 5 to 10 per cent nitrogen.

Coming to urinating we learn "In the course of normal urination the angle formed by a maximum trajectory rarely exceeds 60 degrees from the vertical (with the notable exception of small boys). Accordingly, the angle at which the container should be set lies in the 40-to50 degree range. This is the critical range in that maximum trajectory equals maximum pressure, which in turn equals maximum dispersion and splash."

The men who designed our first public urinals were unaware of these theoretical facts but had great practical experience. So they were able to get the bowls and partitions in the right place. Scientifically the 19th century Geordie urinal was as near perfection as it is possible to make them.

GEORDIE SONG BOOK. Twenty-five of the best Geordie Songs, including Blaydon Races, Keep Yer Feet Still and Dance Te Thy Daddy. Some with music. Illustrated. 64 pages ....

GEORDIE SONGS, JOKES AND RECITATIONS. A collection of local songs with jokes and hilarious recitations ......

THE GEORDIE DICTIONARY. For an explanation of words and usage in Northumberland and Durham.

Early in the 20th century a mishap occured at a public toilet on Tweedmouth docks. The victim was a man called Gardiner. His unfortunate experience was recorded in verse by an engine driver called Grey who was a well known local rhymster. Mr G. D. Bryson, President of the Berwick Amateur Rowing Club says the poem was once a favourite recitation at their annual dinner.

THE SHIT HOUSE ON THE QUAY

There was a man called Gardiner,
At the hour of 10 o'clock,
On the night of the 1st of November
He went across to the dock.

He went to the old tin Shit house
And boldly entered in,
He dropped his nedder garments
And sat down to begin.

Alas a gale was blowing
Upon that fateful day,
It blew the old tin Shit house,
And poor old Bob away.

I went across to Tweedmouth dock,
And saw this total wreck,
And there sat old Bob Gardiner,
With the Shit house round his neck.

A lady who was passing by
Made this exclamation;
"Have they tried to blend the Shit house
with the art of aviation?"

Now he vows they'll have to build him,
A hut more firm and strong,
Before he'll cease from singing,
This most delightful song.

Farewell, Farewell my little hut
No more I'll shit in thee.
For little did I think that night,
That you would shit in me.

THE GEORDIE BOG CO.LTD. Seaton Deleval

THE ORIGINAL

JET
NET

APPROVED BY

W. C. Fields

SHOWROOMS·SHIREMOOR & PITY ME

INTERIOR OF WATER CLOSET AND URINAL CONVENIENCE FOR STREETS AND OTHER PUBLIC SITUATIONS.

Complete, with brass water supply, lamps, and gas fittings.

For 6 Persons, without Urinals,	£64	10	0	For 6 Persons, with Urinal at each end,	£80	0
„ 8 „	84	0	0	„ 8 „	98	10
„ 10 „	98	0	0	„ 10 „	112	0

In the advert for the above toilet we are told that it is enclosed "by a cast iron structure, chaste and elegant in design. The material of which it is composed renders it perfectly impervious to filth and gases, and provision is made for periodically washing the whole by an elastic hose and jet of water. By the thorough means of ventilation adopted, the atmosphere of the interior is kept perfectly fresh, although the Closets alone may be used from eight to ten hundred persons daily".

"*Neddy, Netty,* a certain place that will not bear a written explanation, but which is *depicted to the very life* in a tail-piece in the first edition of Bewick's 'Land Birds' (1797), p.285. In the second edition a bar is placed against the offending part of this *broad* display of native humour."

J. T. Brockett—*A Glossary of North Country Words.* 1825

A larger work by Rev. Oliver Heslop called "Northumberland Words", 1892 omits this common word. What a remarkable growth of hypocrisy during the reign of Victoria.

A fine cast iron toilet from Willington Quay.
To be erected at Beamish Museum.

These cast iron toilets were once found everywhere in the northern counties. They were produced in sections and could be erected in whatever size desired. They were well designed and decorated. Being mass produced they were also comparatively cheap.

PLEASE AVOID URINATION
WHILE THE TRAIN IS STANDING AT
THE STATION

Old Railway Notice

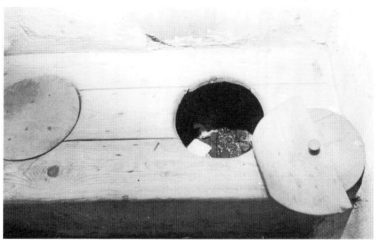

Tanfield Leith Farm—Tantobie
by permission of John Gall

In the gardens of Wallington Hall to the north of the China Pond is an 18th century privy. It was built by Sir Walter Blacket for his personal use. He suffered from a weak bladder but was fond of walking in the garden. The building remains as it was built but the interior has been altered.

FIREMEN LOO-SEN A SEAT

"Young Andrew Curry has got a head for getting to the bottom of things.

Yesterday his curiosity got the better of him—and it took three firemen to loo-sen him from a tight spot.

Because three-year-old Andrew got his head stuck in a toilet seat.

Andrew's mother tried desperately to remove him from the embarrassing position without success so she called the local fire brigade for help.

'He looked a little worried when six big firemen came in It took three of them to ease the seat off using soap.'

'He is fully recovered now—he is just a bit flushed,' she added."

Newcastle Journal – July 1977

THE OLD NEWCASTLE CATTLE MARKET

The public convenience here was a strange arrangement. One farmer suffered the indignity of having his shirt tail pulled under the partition by a "lady" and used as a toilet roll.

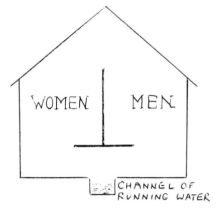

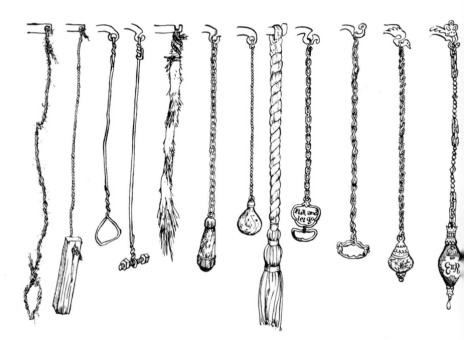

CHAINS

The Geordie netty chains are part of a collection sold recently at Sotherby's for £185,000. According to the special catalogue issued for this important sale the types shown are from left to right:—

Primitive: Advanced Primitive: Unidentified: Industrial: Rural: Utility: Modern: Jacobean: Informative: Bronze Age: Rococo: Jubilee.

The romantic painting showing Bessie Surtees eloping from a
window of the house in Sandhill, now named after her, is well known.
This unique engraving from an old Newcastle Record Book shows
Bessie Surtees house in a different setting. The chamber pots are being
emptied early in the morning. One of the figures on the street is the
Lord Mayor. When they emptied the pots the occupiers were sup-
posed to shout a warning to passers by—*gardy loo*.

The illustration on the cover of this book is a reconstruction by Ronald Embleton of the earliest latrine in Northumbria. The ruins, in a remarkable state of preservation can be seen at Housesteads Roman fort on the Roman Wall. Such latrines are rare in Britain. Charles Daniels in the book *Hadrian's Wall Reconstructed* describes it thus:—

> *"The latrine was behind the rampart at the lowest point of the fort interior, the south-eastern corner, where run-away water from all parts could be canalised to flush it. Practicality of this sort is a well-known Roman characteristic. The seating was placed along the side walls with a stone channel below which was kept clean by frequent flushing from a water tank. Clean water flowed into a floor channel so that the soldiers could wash the sponges which they used instead of paper. This upper channel then emptied into a lower one. In Roman times the walls of the room would have been plastered, so that the stone face would not have been visible. Larger and more elaborate lavatories of this general type are often found attached to the great public baths of the cities of the Empire, but this small building at Housesteads shows that hygiene was as much observed in the forts of the Wall as in the cities of Europe and Africa."*

Acknowledgements

We have received assistance from many people in the writing of the present work. We are particularly indebted to Rosemary Allan and the Beamish Museum who have provided twelve of the illustrations. Dr. W. G. Swan, Roland Bibby of Morpeth, the Northumberland and Newcastle Society, Dick Irwin and Newcastle Reference Library have all provided valuable information. Our artist Susan Martin, G. D. Bryson of Tweedmouth and A. Jensen of Ashington are mentioned in the text. Ronald Embleton has supplied the cover painting and Richard Thompson the cartoons. Norman Brown and Radio Newcastle provided valuable advance publicity and the book has been completed with the two *classic* drawings by Robert Olley.

NO JOB IS COMPLETE
UNTIL THE PAPER WORK
IS DONE

*By permission of
Grant and Iveson*